# THE GIRL WHO DIDN'T KNOW
## *A JOURNEY FROM BOTTOM TO BLOSSOM*

**KYARIS JOHNSON**

Published by Kyaris Johnson

Houston, Texas USA

Copyright © 2018 Kyaris Johnson. All rights reserved.

No part of this book may be reproduced in any form or by any mechanical means, including information storage and retrieval systems without permission in writing from the author, except by a reviewer who may quote passages in a review.

All images, logos, quotes, and trademarks included in this book are subject to use according to trademark and copyright laws of the United States of America.

All Biblical quotations are taken from the American Standard Version
Public Domain

Editing by Kyaris Johnson and Brent Barnett

Cover and Interior Design by Brent Barnett for BeSquaredDesign.com

*This book is dedicated to my angel son, Ryan Augustus Allen II, who in his short eleven months of living gave me all the hope, joy, and love that I needed for my heart to beat again. Ryan, everywhere I go your*

*name will be mentioned.*

*I am leaving footprints for us!*
*Mommy loves you, baby!*

# CONTENTS
INTRODUCTION     5
MOLESTATION 10
THE WAR 21
A LETTER TO EVERYONE WHO STOLE MY INNOCENCE     30
UNPOPULAR     33
DIVORCE 40
A LETTER TO DIVORCE     51
THE TROUBLED RELATIONSHIP     54
LETTER TO THE CHILD I NEVER MET     66
BABY RYAN     68
RYAN'S PASSING     74
RYAN MY SWEET BABY! 83
A LETTER TO MY SIBLINGS     87
A LETTER TO MY MOM     91
A LETTER TO MY STEPMOM     106
ATTENTION     111
SAVED AND SHAPED     115
THE GIRL WHO DIDN'T KNOW - A POEM     123
ABOUT THE AUTHOR     126

# INTRODUCTION

**W**hen people look at me they see compassion, a love for the people, and a smile that never fades. They hear a laugh that is slightly annoying; one that conveys its' own sense of goofiness. People see joy, yet they don't understand my background, obstacles, false perceptions, and the mask that hid my truth and reality. Friends and family have been able to witness my self-discovery, yet there are some things I've never shared with anyone but God. I've been led to share my story multiple times and questioned the impact, influence, and importance my story held. As I shared these thoughts with a good friend, he expressed his opinion of what makes my story an important one to share. The significance of my testimony is my truth. It belongs to me and was given to me by God.

My pain was caused by people, situations, and my own self destruction. I am not proud of everything I'm going to share, but it is my truth, and that truth continues to set me free. As you read the pages of my book, you will see a young woman who never gave up. I pray that my testimony gives you courage to find your truth. When you find that truth, trust God to lead you and to empower you to share with others the strength that your testimony has given you. I am a proud, vocal, unique, vulnerable, and real individual. There is no perfection in what I might say but it's all truth from a woman sharing her journey of brokenness. I am whole today because God is such a good Father, who rebuilt me in His grace, mercy, and love.

As you begin the journey through my testimony, I encourage you to release your mind and your heart so that healing can take place. Life isn't what it should be if adversity protects us from the necessary pain that produces the process of progress and power. I am living proof that God works everything out for your good once you decide to surrender all your cares to Him and lay them at His feet. This book is a series of conversations between God and I and I'm sharing my journey with you.

*Lord, today I sat on the plane watching "The Curious Case of Benjamin Button". As I watched this movie, all I could think about was this dash that most people talk about between the year you were born and the year you perish.*

We all have a purpose, yet the journey is a process. I have been more focused on accomplishing the purpose that I honestly never considered the journey. People often share how proud they are of me, how I inspire them, and how my testimony touches them. It's easy to get caught up in the purpose without realizing the process of being a conqueror through it all. I want to reflect on this journey thus far.

My dash has started to form and what I want you to understand is what that dash represents. It represents love, heartbreak, accomplishments, downfalls, family, accolades, strength, influence, pride, and a heartbeat of life or death. I want my story to be a legacy for my children. I want my life to lead people to God. I pray that this book inspires all of the people who read it to know that God can keep them.

# *MOLESTATION*

*Father, I have found myself moving in life without ever understanding where my strength came from. Thinking back, I found myself trapped in the bondage of someone else's lustful desires which led to molestation. The devil knew that my DNA was like my heavenly Father's. He tried to trick my mind into thinking that my value was wrapped in holding secrets, shedding quiet tears, learning the act of silence, questioning if anyone cares and if I was attracted to women. Wow! Sitting on this plane, my mind is racing with thoughts on how I was trapped, afraid to tell my truth, and of my own reflection. The devil's tricky schemes had me believing nobody would believe my story. I can't believe I'm sitting here crying and reminiscing on thoughts of how my life quickly transitioned into pain.*

I remember wanting someone to save me. How am I this little girl being attacked? Why aren't people noticing that my soul is in bondage and my confidence is dying? Molestation was the first brick in the wall of distance between God and I. This brick was installed by a family member who asked me to play Hide and Seek, which eventually devolved into him coercing me to perform oral sex on him. This was one of many conversations I had with God: *He had a plan to hurt me because he knew that I would say yes to playing. I was a little girl, God. Why wouldn't I want to play an innocent, fun game with a family member? We share the same blood? God, why didn't you stop him?*

Hide and Seek was a game that allowed me to use all these fun and creative methods to find a great hiding place. When I was first introduced to this game, I knew hiding in the basement was the best hiding place. I felt untouchable as I ran down the stairs to hide. I would try to control my breathing and excitement, so I wouldn't be found. I could hear the countdown; 10…9…8…7…6…5…4…3…2…1. I had no clue that the countdown coming to an end was only the beginning of a painful season in my life; a pain that started this perverted mindset. I was five years old giving oral sex to my Cousin. Five years old! I could hear him calling my name and pretending as if he didn't know where I was hiding. My heart fluttered with excitement. He walked into the basement and I covered my mouth trying to be silent. I was caught by the words, *I found you*. I was laughing and abruptly startled that the game came to an end when he grabbed my hair.

I was thrown to the floor and heard him quickly unbuckling his pants while forcing my face towards him to perform oral sex. After he forcefully pulled my hair and unbuckled his pants, he then placed his penis into my mouth. I was rendered completely silent. His moans of pleasure and my groans of pain were the soundtrack to a horrific moment that would forever change my life. After he finished molesting me, I was told to go upstairs. Trying to process what had just happened to me, I sat in another Cousin's room as I nearly drowned in the pain of my encounter. Hide and Seek became a game I didn't want to play anymore, but I was still forced to continue giving him oral sex. I was young, but I knew that what was happening to me, wasn't right. The devil began placing thoughts of fear in my mind. Satan wanted me to believe that telling anyone about what I had experienced would get me in trouble.

*God, why didn't you stop the pain that broke down my spirit? God, what gets me is that not only didn't You stop the pain, You allowed two more people to take advantage of me. Is that the way You show Your love for me?*

My parents are both from the Midwest; my Father being from Detroit, and my Mother hailing from Cincinnati. My parents would leave me with my amazing Grandma, who loved me so much. When my Grandma would leave the house to run errands, my Aunt would stay to watch me. One day as my Aunt and I were sitting on the couch, I found myself becoming her prey. My Aunt crawled on top of me and started to rock back and forth, dry humping me. The thoughts that overcame me in these moments are hard to describe, even after all of these years.

*God, why does everyone want to hurt me?*

As I watched the faces of my abusers taking sick enjoyment in victimizing me, I began to drift deeper into silence. I did not understand how they could ignore my pain. How could my Aunt want to fondle my body and then pretend as if nothing happened when our family was around?

*Lord, my Lord; why have You forsaken me?*

I had not even reached my tenth birthday and my innocence had been stolen. My mind was filled with these impure sexual thoughts that were more than I could understand or could handle.

*Lord, I know You know that I struggle with wondering if I could possibly like girls. Why is that when I see other young girls walk past me and I look at their bodies,*

*I'm led to impure thoughts?*

My Father worked for General Motors and because of his job our family relocated to Texas. As you will later discover, Texas is where most of my pain happened. My parents have big hearts and family means a lot to them. My parents would open their home to family members in need, which I always found amazing. One of my Cousins from Michigan who was the younger Brother of my first molester, was seeking a second chance in life and moved into our family home. Initially, having him in the house worked well. He was cool, and the living arrangement was fun because it was like having an older Brother. I trusted him. One day, my Cousin wanted to wrestle. I was an extreme tom-boy so fighting was more fun to me than most other activities. As he slammed me around, I started laughing loudly.

The wrestling quickly turned into our bodies being tangled up, with him on top of me and his hand on my private area. My heart stopped for a moment and I began to wonder if he was like the others. Was this wrestling game merely a setup to hurt me? He started to apply pressure with his hands and his breathing reminded me of the other two family members who had abused me. He, too, seemed to lose himself inside of a moment of perverted pleasure as he preyed on me.

My molester Cousin had some very odd ways about how he carried himself. His behavior was extreme, bold, and sneaky all at the same time. Not only was he physically abusing my innocence, but he also exposed me to porn and objectified me sexually. I tried every method of avoiding the abuse including having my little brother sleep with me, and sleeping in open areas like in our game room. I gave my best effort to protect myself, but all of my evasive measures didn't stop the abuse. He watched me as I showered and as I slept.

*God, this was the time that I needed you the most.*

*I was terrified, and I couldn't find You. I prayed,*

*asking You to stop it and it only got worse.*

You may be wondering why I didn't tell. I didn't tell anyone because my Cousin threatened to hurt my sister if I exposed him, and as an older sister I wanted to protect her. I was also still dealing with the question of whether or not people would believe me. The devil had me tricked into thinking it was my fault. I began to ask God questions regarding this situation.

*Where are You God? Don't You remember while I was in class with tears falling from my eyes as I wrote in my journal, ways to share this information with my parents? I was living in the house with my molester and my parents had no clue. My baby sister knew because she walked in on him, but I begged her not to tell.*

*Fear killed every ounce of joy my heart held. Lord,*

*I just wanted You to step in.*

*I wanted You to save me. Why didn't You?*

# THE WAR

From the ages of Five to Fourteen years old, I faced an ongoing battle of my body being abused by family members. I dealt with the struggle of not being able to explain what was happening to me and why it was wrong. I didn't fully understand that I had been molested. I did not clearly understand that I was not at fault. The devil had me held in bondage of my secret, causing me to not share my truth.

I remember the night I decided to finally share my truth and how it all played out. I wanted to go to a party, but my parents were very protective and wouldn't allow me to attend. I immediately got an attitude when my parents rejected my request. They made it clear that their reason for saying that I could not go was because they wanted to protect me. Seeing my facial expression caused my Dad to question me. It was as if he could read my mind and he began to ask me a variety of questions to understand the meaning of my facial expression. He immediately asked me "Kyaris, has someone touched you?" We were in the living room with my siblings upstairs, and the Cousin who was molesting me at the time was in the kitchen. He was wearing headphones and had no clue of the conversation that was taking place in the living room.

As my Dad awaited my answer, my Baby Sister leaned over the banister and said, "Kyaris, if you don't tell, I will". My entire body went numb. My sister clearly wanted a response sooner than I could give one. Before I could blink, she yelled, "Kyaris has been touched by our Cousin". The house immediately turned into a war-zone. Tears, aggressive tones and body gestures, and emotions that couldn't be held back. The scene was chaotic. My Father grabbed a baseball bat with rage in his eyes, ready to kill my Cousin. My Mother was screaming and crying. All I could do was run across the street to a friend's house to get away from the pain that I had just caused my family. Instead of feeling free because the truth was out, I had now taken on the guilt of sharing my truth. My Dad was at war with his family, and I felt it was all my fault.

My parents started fighting, and I felt like all this destruction was completely my fault. This was the beginning of creating an emotional mask that I would wear for years to follow. I pushed my feelings deep into myself, and I worried about what others thought of me. Thoughts raced through my mind: *I've destroyed my family. God, You allowed me to take on a guilt that really didn't belong to me.*

I remember falling into a deep black hole that night. No one even realized that Kyaris Johnson was lost, living a false identity, afraid to be herself, and afraid to embrace her pain. I made my way back to the house and went straight to my room. My parents checked on me and decided that I needed group counseling. I wasn't ready for this and wanted everyone to stop talking for a moment, so that I could scream, cry, be mad, and feel all the pain that had made me numb. My parents were broken themselves but wanted me to heal through a counseling class with other women. I didn't know any of the women in that class. They thought that sharing my brokenness in a group setting was the only answer to my healing. I wanted my parents to look in my eyes with compassion. I wanted their love to connect to my soul and see that darkness had overtaken my joy. As much as I wanted these things, my parents couldn't give them to me because they were also broken. The pain that took over my life that night made me fall into a deep depression. I felt rejected, embarrassed, and soiled. I didn't trust anyone. I was angry because I wanted people to help me a certain type of way. When they didn't, the devil planted seeds that no one cared, and I deemed them as selfish and unloving.

My heart had entered a search of wanting to be found and loved. The atmosphere in my life changed for the worse. The guilt I took on because I wanted to protect my family made the atmosphere even more unbearable. The chaos that came with sharing the events that took place with one of my molesters left me vulnerable and too ashamed to tell my whole truth.

I didn't share the part about being molested by two other family members with my parents until I was about seventeen years old. This was because the reaction I received from my family after being open about one of my molesters pushed me into a depressive state.

Once again, I donned the mask that had become a way of protecting myself from the pain I felt. I pretended like I was fine and tried to move on from the pain that was always haunting me. I would always tell people I was fine but would not even make eye contact with them. I had masked my pain by excelling at sports. The more I achieved, the less people would ask about my personal life. I tried to be normal but normal to me had become a mask I used to hide myself from others. And I used it to trick myself as well. I wanted to believe that I was okay but I wasn't.

I discovered that I was addicted to porn and would often be in class thinking perverted thoughts. The crazy part is that I didn't want to have sex. I was afraid and the thought of having someone on top of me brought flash backs. Memories I didn't want re-surfacing.

*God, not once did You make yourself known. You just left me alone to fight this battle. You are truly at fault because You are known as the creator. Why didn't You paint a life for me that was pretty and sparkly? My life was dark yet covered up with a little shimmer. People saw a false reality of my life and I want to thank You for being a God who shows favoritism and selective love.*

*God, You have forsaken me and allowed my life to be controlled by the devil. Up to this point, my life has been a story of pain that people will never understand. We all have stories, right? No need to even share that I am broken because it's not like You care. God, I want You to know that when I mentioned that I didn't trust anyone, I was including You.*

# A LETTER TO EVERYONE WHO STOLE MY INNOCENCE

I used to wonder how you could hurt me and still live with yourself. How could you hurt me and yet have conversations with my parents as if life was good and you weren't abusing their child? I really hated all of you and I always wondered what would happen when I came face-to-face with you as an adult. I wondered if I would boss up and be ready to catch a round or two with you, or would I be overly dramatic and scream, *I hate you.* I wondered if I would go off on you and walk off leaving you broken by my words. It all felt good inside when I thought about it, but I never got up the courage to do any of it.

*God, You are such a healer and I'm grateful.*

I wrote letters to you to release my pain. Afterwards, I took those letters to the trash can in front of my sister's leasing office, tore them up, and released myself from the pain. I have forgiven each of you and my heart wants nothing more than for all of you to forgive yourselves. I remember God saying to me that forgiving is to free yourself but to also release your brother and sister from the bondage the devil is trying to keep them in. I realized I had to stop calling you molesters. You are children of Christ but the act you participated in was molestation. My heart wants you to be free and I will not hold you in bondage when God has freed me. I love you and my prayers are lifted for you all.

## **ASSIGNMENT:**

I ask that you take a moment, a deep breath, and grab a piece of paper. Play this song: *Gracious Tempest* by Hillsong and Free. Allow your heart to soak in God's love. Don't be in a rush to write or get up. Allow your pain and anger to rise up and pour out in a scream, shed tears, pray and surrender it all to God. When the Holy Spirit leads you. pick up your pen, forgive yourself, forgive others, and forgive God for He never left your side. I am with you in prayer. Let's release the darkness the devil has tried to keep us trapped in and show everyone who hurt us, God's love.

*You can do it!*

## *UNPOPULAR*

*Lord, we don't have to talk about this too long, but I find it crazy that I was an unpopular person but popular at the same time. I wanted to fit in so bad that I found myself in more drama because I desired to be accepted and tried to be cool. I wanted to be like the pretty girl, Hannah Johnson. She was super pretty and a model. I was short, skinny, didn't have the best clothes, and I was a tomboy. God, do You remember when I stole my mom's heels and thought I was going to be sexy, and cool? Well, You already know what happened when I arrived at school. I almost broke my neck trying to walk in them. I remember wanting the attention of one boy, for people to be my friend, and being the girl, everyone loved. Instead. I was the girl nobody liked, and the girl people talked about.*

In high school, I was such a great athlete that people would make me feel bad because I had a Father who invested in me. I had parents who wanted to see me win. I was also a girl who was willing to sacrifice the fun life to have a future. Yet, other kids made me feel terrible about my gifts. In my Junior year, some of the popular girls would send text messages to each other with comments about me that were lies, saying that I was gay and impure. They talked about my family, the mole I have on my face and how it grows hair out of it. Yes, my mole grows long and curly pieces of hair. *God, You could have left the hair out even though it's something I grew to love.* Those messages and small talk killed whatever confidence that was left in me. I wanted more than anything, to be popular because it looked like success.

What I discovered was that being popular meant portraying an image that wasn't true. Being popular meant broken and lost people hurting other broken and lost people. People didn't know that I was hurting, that I was being molested every day I went home, that I had to boil water at the neighbor's house just to shower, I was watching my parents sacrifice for me, and I was watching my parent's marriage fall apart. My classmates created rumors instead of asking me how I was doing and who I really was. I could easily make up an excuse for their behavior, charging it to their age and lack of maturity, because of how bad I wanted to be accepted.

I wanted and needed someone to like me, and to love me. I wanted to be cool and was so focused on becoming cool that I failed classes trying to perfect stupidity. Why? I still don't have the answers to that one. Could it be because the devil took away my confidence as a child? Was it because the attention I received at home was based on my ability to play sports and my future? Or was it because I just wanted to be like everyone else? I guess it's a little bit of everything.

## ASSIGNMENT:

Grab some sticky notes. Sit at your counter, on the floor, or any area where you can place a mirror in front of you. Please make three sections on your mirror. The left section will be what the enemy has told you about yourself. Understand that bullying has nothing to do with you but the spirit that is stirring inside of the bully planted by the devil. Write down every negative word given. In the middle section, write down what God says about you. Ask the Holy Spirit to lead you to scripture and to help you get started, I am sharing a few with you:

*Psalm 139:14 God says, "...I am fearfully and wonderfully made."*

*Zechariah 2:8 God says, " ... for He that toucheth you toucheth the apple of His eye."*

*Deuteronomy 7:6 God says, "...(I have) hath chosen thee to be a people for (My) own possession."*

In the last section, write down what you think about yourself. As time passes, and you begin to stop believing the lie the devil has fed you, take off one of the sticky notes and replace it with a freedom word. Here is a list of words but focus on the words that God will give you. ***Joy, love, peace, compassion, beautiful, grace, mercy, intelligent, humble, meek, amazing, loved, creative, and victorious.***

Meditate on these words and compare them to the middle section. This will give you a clear picture of how ugly the devil really is. He wants you to believe something that God never said about you or who He created you to be. In the end, trust God's word and His promises about you.

# *DIVORCE*

*Lord, why did people believe they understood me because we were classmates, peers, or teammates? They didn't have a clue that I was being raised by both parents and that our house was full of chaos and brokenness. How can two young parents who are still trying to find themselves raise children when they were still teens themselves?*

My parents were very young and honestly did the best that they could do. They made many sacrifices for my siblings and I. My parents pushed out the best in me, so I wouldn't end up in the same position as them. I knew that they wanted us to have everything that they didn't have but growing up was still a struggle.

My family lived in a middle-class neighborhood with finances that did not match middle-class living. I remember hearing the arguments about money often. I remember taking on more guilt as I watched my parents give me everything they had in order for me to play sports. They wanted me to go to college and have a chance at life. My parents borrowed money, sold items, and we would even go to our neighbor's house just to boil water to take showers. We lived in a nice size house, but the inside of the house was decorated with secrets, tears, pain, and heartbreak.

My Father was the leader of our household. He gave me love, attention, and I knew that he would always be there for me. My Dad was my basketball coach and my best friend. He was also my biggest supporter and critic. My Father was great at being my Dad, but he wasn't the best example of a husband. My Dad held a lot of anger and hurt inside. He took on this mentality that black men shouldn't cry. I never saw my Dad cry as a child, but I witnessed his anger and aggressive actions more than I wanted to. *Lord, I remember crying to You because I witnessed my Dad with two different personalities that I just couldn't understand it.* How could my Father who would paint my toes and tell me how great I was, be the same person who hurt the woman who gave birth to me?

How could my Daddy who never missed basketball games, track meets, or school functions, be the same man who would have such aggressive ways? He was aggressive with my Mother but after time, his aggressiveness became an attack throughout the entire household. My Dad appeared to be trapped mentally, trying to break free, but his bondage to the enemy hurt others. I love my Dad, but I was afraid of him. He placed a fear inside of me because I didn't understand the behaviors he portrayed. *This is not how a Dad is supposed to be,* I thought. *God, I just remember wanting my Dad to be nice all the time.* I remember being afraid because I didn't know what mood he would be in. I was young, and we didn't have many conversations about emotions, stress, pressure, or the reasons why I witnessed him become two different men all the time.

My Mother, on the other hand, has a big heart. She is very creative with a heart that is always willing to help others. I wasn't as close to my Mother growing up, but never questioned that she loved and supported me. My Mother was always excited to help me with projects, school dances, and she wouldn't take any mess if someone was cheering against me. My Mother was delightful but broken. Her love and life were wrapped up in her children and husband. My Mother appeared weak to me when I was a child. There were many times when I witnessed my Mom take verbal, mental, physical, and emotional abuse from my Father. I didn't see her strength at all.

*God, I remember asking You why does she allow this?*

*Why won't she leave?*

I remember being afraid for my Mother. However, her role as a wife, was not one that I admired. I knew that a wife was to take care of the home. That wasn't the case in our house. My Mother loved us and her husband, but she didn't take on the full role as a wife. I had the impression that a wife was a woman who voluntary became a doormat. As I watched my mother and other women in their roles as wives, I began to believe that the priority of a wife was to please her husband; even if that mean losing one's self. I remember my Dad being mad at basic things like meals weren't cooked or the house wasn't clean, so I kept that in mind. Honestly, I didn't know what a good husband or wife looked like so imagining a Godly husband or wife was far off my radar.

My parents were young, and the devil used that against them. I could only imagine how their minds were running. The lack of wisdom and understanding of marriage, not being complete as individuals, financially unstable, and raising four kids had to bring chaos into their lives. My Father now had the role of being a leader but couldn't supply every need for his family comfortably. My Mother desired to be a great wife, but she wasn't whole and did not have any direction. It was hard to witness two great people wanting to do right but not having the tools to complete the vision they had for their family.

*God, can You see why I was so mad at You?*

I was being molested at the same time I witnessed both of my parents hurting each other. I took on a lot being the older sibling to my younger sister and two younger brothers, I wasn't sure if I was upholding my role either. I remember my peers thinking we had it all. They saw a nice house and both of my parents supporting me. They had no clue that my home was a living hell. I hated going home, so the gym became my outlet. I could work out all night because it allowed me the opportunity to avoid the drama at home and to avoid becoming someone's sexual victim.

Then, the ugly divorce happened. My Mother questioning my Dad about cheating and my Dad questioning my Mother about her role as a wife. Our house became one scary place. As I witnessed both of my parents on their last cord, I was afraid to say anything wrong. Our house exhibited no love. I never saw my parents kiss or show affection towards one another the entire time they were together. Now don't get me wrong, they clearly were doing something. They had four children.

Our house became a dead zone. My parents were roommates instead of living like a married couple that loved each other. The divorce was hard for me because I had never lived without my Dad being in the house and my Mom was broken to her core. I am a runner and I ran my way into the arms of young man who became the void filler in my life.

Our relationship was for all the wrong reasons but… *God, can we discuss that later?*

*You see God, it was hard to believe in You because I felt that You could have changed their hearts. You could have brought them back together. God, my parents displayed a marriage that did not inspire me. All I witnessed was struggle and animosity in their marriage. Broken people trying to make it work so that their children could have a chance. They wanted to give us what they didn't have but honestly Lord, this was a generational curse that was working its way into my life.*

*God, how can a person be a good parent but stay in an unhealthy marriage?*

What I witnessed led to a negative mindset on relationships.

*Lord, do You know how much I struggled watching both parents being victims of one another?*

My life was dysfunctional but, yet it became normal to me. How could I develop a healthy understanding of love when the meaning of love registered as broken people who hurt broken people?

# *A LETTER TO DIVORCE*

*I bind and rebuke the spirit the has attached itself to families who serve the Lord. Unity will be our portion and divorce will be a bad joke that no one pays attention to anymore. Jesus, I lift up a prayer to you covering every reader who has considered divorce, who are happily married, or who have been affected by divorce.*

*Divorce will not gain victory in our homes. Divorce will not cause any more damage. Strongholds are broken, patience, understanding, and joy are released. Generational curses are broken, and freedom is covering us from carrying on the mentality that marriages never work out and are nothing but contracts. Help us understand Lord, that marriage is a covenant.*

*God, today I release Your Glory over marriages and the unity of becoming one with one another. Women will be gentle but not blinded to thinking that gentle means weak. Men will understand that leading doesn't mean controlling. Love is not a choice but a command. Lord have Your way in the marriages across the world. In Jesus' name I pray, Amen.*

## ASSIGNMENT:

Write down what you witnessed about marriage growing up. How did your family view marriage? Was marriage looked at as a partnership or more like roommates? Were you an eyewitness to a marriage that was a representation of God's Covenant? If you were raised in a single-parent home, was there co-parenting outside of the home?

With your upbringing and the examples of marriage you witnessed, how did it affect your life and past relationships? Now study what God teaches on marriage and write a letter to the marriage you see in your future.

## *THE TROUBLED RELATIONSHIP*

*Sweet Jesus! Life is only getting harder for me. My parents are going through a divorce, our home is broken, my family who lives in Michigan has stopped talking to me, my immediate family has no clue, how bad I am hurting, and my body has been violated by other family members. Lord, I will not forget how I wanted to be so popular in high school. I wanted attention, but I was so afraid and shy that I opted to stay to myself. I used my engagement in sports to live the life I thought I wanted. I remember my first boyfriend. Lord, he was everything I believed I deserved but clearly, I didn't know my own worth. I later discovered that I just wanted someone to love me and see me for whom I was.*

I asked my parents if I could date, and they agreed.

My mom made me sign a contract with affirmations like: you won't forget that you exist; you won't forget that you're a queen; you won't have sex. I signed it out of pure excitement, knowing that I would be able to date someone who seemed to care for me. The beginning of our relationship was great. I stayed focused, our parents supported us being together, and we cared about each other. See I had never been in a relationship and the only model I had was my parents. I found myself loving him more than I loved myself and I wanted to be everything he desired.

The day I lost my virginity was the day I lost myself. I became a doormat to what he wanted from our relationship. I loved him so much, that our relationship became unhealthy. I slowly stopped enjoying basketball because I wanted to spend as much time with him as possible. I stopped growing as a young woman because I feared outgrowing my boyfriend or him becoming envious. *Lord, I do remember being at church and crying, trying to find You.* I feared what my boyfriend would think because I wasn't familiar on how to pray or worship. I thought I looked stupid and I found myself becoming the woman of my worse dreams. I was so in love that I couldn't stay true to who I knew I needed to be. I was tasting the struggle my mom went through.

This soul-tie was wrapped up in an unhealthy relationship that was controlled by lust, being insecure, and developing a needy spirit. I felt like I had to be the Shero in the relationship to make it work and prove to myself that I could be wifey material one day. I was sixteen years old and washing clothes, doing homework, and other things, pretending to be a wife. Arguing with him like I was a grown woman. I was seeking validation from a young man who was broken himself. I knew I was caught up in the generational curse of poor relationships. I was looking at him like a Father figure because he displayed some of the same traits as my Dad. His personality switched up often. He was loving to others and to me on certain days and then he would change into a person who was full of anger. Sound familiar, Lord?

A couple of years later life took another turn. My Mother had me take a pregnancy test and guess what? Yes, the test was positive. The relationship only became worse when I found out that I was pregnant, even though, in all honesty, we had planned on getting pregnant. My mind was in a state of confusion. I was so eager to be a great wife that I matured faster than I should have. I wanted to have something that brought me love but my mom wasn't buying it. She was so angry and the last thing on her mind was becoming a Grandmother. I called my then boyfriend so that I could update him on the news. As he pulled up to my house, I ran up to the car to share that I was pregnant. I remember we were both excited. My Mom, on the other hand, showed no excitement. In fact, she immediately forced me to abort my unborn child within the same week. I was angry with everyone including myself and wondered why I didn't stand stronger on what I believed. The same day I had the abortion, I was forced to go to basketball practice. I felt that this was way too soon but I really didn't have a say in the matter. I would have these dreams of little fingers touching my hand and then blood overpowering the situation. I kept hearing the noise of the vacuum that crushed my child.

Once again, what mattered to me didn't seem to matter to others. Everyone just moved forward in their daily activities as my life was falling into a deep black hole. I had so many thoughts of suicide.

As time goes on a year later to be exact, I slowly matured and realized that I wanted to enjoy life as a single young woman. I signed a scholarship to play college basketball and Lord, I was excited for a new chapter. I broke up with my boyfriend but kept the benefits of sex. I remember one night we were having sex and I thought to myself, something isn't right! Reality kicks in during a track meet where I became very sick and tired from running a mile which was my bread and butter. That something that was not right had a lot to do with how I was eating chocolate bars, hot dogs, and drinking pop all together. I knew that if I was pregnant, there was no way I was going to share it with anyone this time. My sister and I pretty much had this cycle system that when I ended, she started, well hers ended, and I hadn't started. Lord Jesus, I am pregnant again, was all I could say.

## TO THE EX

Thank you because now I know better. I didn't know my worth nor did I realize that I carried behaviors from my parent's brokenness into our relationship. You helped me realize that I needed time to developed inner strength and new norms. You also helped me realize that I will never settle for less or be taken for granted. This trial and error experience helped me to develop, and will ultimately benefit my future husband and family.

## TO THE SISTER STRUGGLING WITH THE EX

Wish them the best and prepare yourself through Christ for the man who fears God. One that will love you as Christ loves the church and be gentle and strong enough to submit. Break-ups can be difficult. I struggled to separate my emotions from my ex and could never understand why. Was he a terrible person? No, but we were young and didn't know who we were through God's eyes. My sister, it's ok to cry because this is a form of grief. There is no time limit on how long it takes for you to heal a broken heart. Just remember that you must keep moving. Every day, thank God for another day. Get up, dress up and show up to look better than you feel. See yourself through God's eyes and through this beautiful journey called life. You're going to be ok and I pray joy and peace over your life.

## ASSIGNMENT:

As an undergrad, I remember my mentor giving me an assignment that blessed my life. I want to share it with you.

Write down all the names of people you have dated even if it was a one-night stand, a free dinner, or an occasional relationship. Then, write down the physical and internal traits they carried that attracted you to them. Now, examine the list to determine what traits you are commonly attracted to. In your own words, define what each trait means to you. Next, write down your Mother's and your Father's traits to see if they mimic the common traits you experienced in your relationships. Last, but not least, write down the traits of Jesus and examine your lists. Do your traits mirror what Jesus represents? If not, ask God to give you a heart check to help you understand why you are attracted to these traits. Then ask God to release you from the understanding of wrong love.

*Example:* When I was writing my list, I noticed that a common trait I was attracted to, was a dominate one. When I defined what strong looked like for me, it was controlling. I was attracted to men who controlled me, and I saw that as a form of love as opposed to insecurities running through our blood. God taught me what a protector was and released me from being attracted to someone who was possessive and controlling.

# *LETTER TO THE CHILD I NEVER MET*

My Dearest Child Whom I Never Met:

I was sixteen years old and I didn't know how to speak up for myself. I was selfish for wanting to create you as a void filler to heal the pain I had encountered over the years. Sorry will never be enough to express how I truly feel. This letter can't make up for the decision I made. I've always wondered if you were a girl or boy. If you looked like me, and what your personality would have been like. Would I have been a great mom? I remember hearing your heart beat and breaking down at the thought of what was about to happen next. I remember sleepless nights and painful moments of hating myself. What I want you to know my son or daughter, is that I am your mommy. I will always love you and you will forever be in my heart. We never met but we will always be connected.

## ASSIGNMENT:

I wish I had one for you, but I don't. Healing from my abortion came from the Holy Spirit filling my womb with peace as I lifted my hands, fell to my knees and cried from my womb for help.

# BABY RYAN

*Lord, being pregnant at seventeen years old after a recent abortion was something I didn't know how to deal with.*

At this point in my life, I wasn't ready to be pregnant again. I was preparing for college and wasn't expecting this kind of news. After looking at the pregnancy test there was no excitement like the first time, but I will say that I refused to have another abortion. I had my mind made up that I was going to fight for my child and give him or her the life they deserved. The pain I felt aborting the first child that God blessed me with was something I couldn't experience again. I was about to graduate high school and I knew that I had to take responsibility for my actions.

Although I knew that being pregnant would be tougher this time, I was ready for the journey. I recently had signed a college scholarship to play basketball and people spoke negative comments about me once the news spread that I was pregnant. The comments were things like "I knew it"; "What a waste of talent"; "You did what all girls can do which is lay on your back"; and "Now, you're just another statistic." I was scared but I knew that my child was going to have an amazing life. These words broke my spirit, but I just tried to block them out of my memory. I tried to hide my pregnancy but morning sickness and ill-fitting clothes gave it away.

The baby's Father and I weren't on speaking terms, so I found myself going to doctor appointments by myself and crying a lot. When I discovered that I was going to have a son, I was elated but found myself venting to my best friend during math class about my pregnancy. The conversation quickly led to a breakdown of tears, questions, and anger of why I felt like I was going to be raising my son by myself.

This part is crazy! I was so controlled by negative love that I only named my son Ryan because his Father said if I didn't then he knew he wasn't the Dad. I knew I had only been with him, but the fear of my son being without a Father trapped me into giving my son a name I didn't agree with. My pregnancy wasn't easy at all, to say the least. At this point in my life my Dad was barely around, my Mother was mad, and the baby's Father was nowhere to be found. The brokenness continued, and did I mention I found out during my first blood test that I tested positive for pregnancy and chlamydia. My life was just moving, and I was lost.

Ryan had now been born and was a super energetic child who put my body through unexplainable pain during the pregnancy. Ryan was so adorable. From the moment he looked into my eyes, I knew that my life belonged to him. *You made Ryan perfect, God.* My life as I had known it had changed forever. I surrendered my young adult enjoyment so that I could give my newborn baby a future.

Finishing college was the only way I knew that would open doors for me to become a Mother who could give her son everything he needed. I had a plan. I would attend college in Texas so that I could drive home often. My mom would take care of my son during my time in school and this way, he could also be around his Dad and the rest of our family. I knew that if I sacrificed the next four years to finish college, I would be equipped to give my son a lifetime of accomplished hopes and dreams.

I was excited for my baby boy and the amazing future I desired for us. College was going well, and my peers knew everything about my son. Whenever it was time to drive home, all I could think about was seeing him and his smile. It made me glow. Ryan presented a love that I needed; an unconditional love that saw past all of my flaws. Ryan was my motivation and he encouraged me to live for both of us. Ryan changed my heart and brought joy to my soul. His smile, loving laugh, energetic ways, and his hugs were the things that melted my heart. Ryan Augustus Allen saved me! He saved me from falling into depression, giving up on myself, and losing my way. I regained my joy.

# RYAN'S PASSING

*Father God, You never warned me how life could change in the blink of an eye. And then it happened. Lord, this is the hardest thing for me to talk about.*

This moment turned me into a woman people couldn't recognize. More importantly, a woman I couldn't recognize. On October 3, 2012 around 1:00pm as I was in class, I received news that my eleven-month-old son was in ICU and that he was in critical condition. I quickly was out of the classroom onto the campus ground sprinting to my dorms but before I could make it, I remember losing my breath in the middle of the volleyball sandpit and was carried out by my teammate into my Coach's office.

As I was sitting in the office, my coach enters the room, he bends down to meet me at eye level to tell me that Ryan Allen the son who grew in my belly, who was cut out of my stomach, and trusted me to protect him was GONE. How could this happen? What went wrong? I sat in the chair with a blank, concerned face. My heart was crushed and writing this part of my story makes me feel sick to my stomach. I had just received news that my son, my baby, my heart was no longer with us anymore.

My coaches were generous in flying me to Arlington, Texas so that I could be there for my son. I was picked up at that the airport by my uncle and I remember him driving in a different direction than where the hospital was located. I asked him where we were going, and he said he was taking me to my Dad's house. Out of frustration I asked another question.

"Why aren't we going to the hospital?", I asked my Uncle. He answered, "Because Ryan isn't there." I was extremely confused and furious at this point and could have fought anyone in my path. I wanted to scream but instead, I temporarily detached from my emotions.

Hours later after getting to my Father's house, I still wasn't sure what exactly had happened! My family felt it was best for my Mother and I to meet face to face. We went to my best friend's house which was good because their family was close to ours. As I was sitting across from my Mom waiting on someone to tell me the entire story as to what happened to my son. My Mother finally opened up and begins to tell me that she left my son in the bathtub and that he had drowned. Lord, No! I remember wanting to flip the table over that separated us but decided against it. Although I hadn't given my life to God at this point, He still covered my mind. I then remember saying to my Mom, "It's okay, and I forgive you", but internally, I was angry, and I blamed her. Looking back, I'm pleased that I wasn't honest with my feelings towards my Mom because the Devil would have attacked her more.

I knew Ryan was gone but I wanted to see my son one last time. I was a teenage girl getting ready to plan a funeral for my eleven-month-old son. I intended to do as much as I could during the days before Ryan's funeral, feeling that this was my last chance to cherish him. Some days went by before the funeral arrangements began, and word had begun to spread that Ryan had passed. The pain of my Son's death caused me to isolate myself; leaving my phone with missed calls, unanswered text messages, and voicemails that I had no intention of listening to.

The time came to pick out the casket. I had only been to two funerals in my life up to that point. I could not understand how I even arrived at a place where I was flipping through a casket catalog at 19. I was not browsing Eastbay for his football gear. I was not looking at pictures of smiling students strolling across the quad to help him select the right college. I was not even helping him circle possible Christmas gifts in the Big Toy Book. I was choosing a casket for my child.

Once I had chosen a casket, I was brought in to see the body of my son for the first time. He was laying there, swollen, a darker skin complexion, purple lips, and his curly hair was stiff from the autopsy. I went home that day thinking that my life was over. Contemplating both the wake and funeral was becoming too much for me. I was lost in pain trying to smile and show others that I was strong when really, I had hit rock bottom. How did my life come to this?

On the day of the funeral, I wore a white dress with blue heels and dressed my son in a white tuxedo with his cute little blue hat that had anchors on it. At the gravesite, his Dad and I were given blue balloons to release and I remember having the hardest time. Releasing a balloon was a symbolization of giving my son to God. Although I eventually made it a tradition to release blue balloons to celebrate my Son's birthday, I still had a difficult time coping with it all. I didn't believe in God anymore because I wasn't ready to let go of my Son. I hated God, myself, my Mother, his Dad and everyone in general.

*Lord, this moment was so hard for me to understand.*

People would often ask me If I was okay and then would say I know your Mom is really hurting. Hello! I wanted to tell them, do you remember she left him in the tub? I am his Mother and the one who is hurting. I knew they meant well with their sympathy, but they never lost a child and it made me want to scream at their comments. Instead, I kept the emotions bottled up inside and chose to smile and agree with them. I hated everyone at this moment. My beautiful blessing was six feet under at eleven months of age and my mom and I had become enemies. I felt so many emotions about my mom.

I didn't see this situation as a Mother versus daughter but a Mother versus Mother. I couldn't look at her and see a Mother. I had anger in my heart because my son was not with me. I bottled all my pain inside and the devil was winning at this moment by keeping me in bondage to my pain. The circumstance planted hate, but the devil watered it nicely with guilt, more hate, an unforgiving spirit, and many other feelings. That day I lost three people; my son, my Mother, and myself.

## *RYAN MY SWEET BABY!*

Ryan Allen, I miss you and I pray that you are proud of me.

I remember the last day that we played together. I had you in a wagon pushing you down the street as the wind slapped you hard in the face. The look on your face was priceless. I remember when you would fake cough just to get my attention. I remember how you slept in a ball like I still do. How you smiled and loved everyone. You are my baby of joy and I miss you. I promised you that I would finish what I started, and I kept that promise. I was determined to finish that degree, no matter how long it took me, and guess what?

Mommy did it! Losing you Ryan was so hard. After you died I felt like I couldn't do anything right, but I found strength to continue, even amidst the crazy chaos and depression.

Ryan, I remember walking to class with thoughts of giving up until I looked down and saw your name paved into the concrete, (At Texas Southern University in-between Courtyard and the Student Center the name Ryan is paved in the ground.). It was just the reminder I needed to recognize that I was not on this journey of finding myself alone. You were right there with me. Whenever I wanted to give up, I would go to that place to see your name and my heart automatically warmed up with encouragement. I miss you so much and there's not a day that goes by that I don't cherish our memories.

My Son, my sweet baby. I love you and I can't wait to see you when I get to the pearly gates. I know that you and Jesus are having the best time. Not having you around is still hard because I anticipated the years of watching you grow up. I wanted to cheer you on as you played sports, watch with excitement and joy as you started your first day of school, give you a dollar to put in the tithing bucket. Boy, there's so much I still imagine.

People ask me all the time how I healed from your death, but the only answer I have is that you were God's plan to save me! Your life brought me joy and your death brought me to Jesus. I love you, Baby Ryan.

## A LETTER TO MY SIBLINGS

*Lord, my Baby Sister KiMyah tried to connect with me on the day that I lost baby Ryan. That day my Sister felt pain and I ignored her feelings. Timing is everything and I should have been there for her. I have always been a woman who ran from her problems. I was shy of confrontation and I hated facing my pain. I could make up so many excuses on why I ignored my Sister, but the truth is, Jesus hung on the cross and forgave a sinner in amid this own pain. so, what makes me exempt from being there for my Sister?*

To my siblings KiMyah, Kimani, Kaleb and Breona; please forgive me for the pain I caused you and the negative things I taught you.

There were times when I was so wrapped up in the world and my own pain that I wasn't there for you. KiMyah, we are only three years apart and we have always been close. I felt as though I've failed you and haven't been the perfect example of a woman for you to model. I introduced you to pornography after someone who hurt me, introduced it to me. I planted a sexual seed in you that I have to take responsibility for. I ignored your feelings and I neglected to encourage you the way you encouraged me. KiMyah, I am so proud of the young woman, Wife, Sister, Daughter, Student, and hard worker you are. You are truly my best friend. Kimani, we never spoke much about this, but you mentioned to me that your picture wasn't in Ryan's obituary and I am sorry. I wasn't in charge of the pictures, but I should have taken to heart, what was your concern and poured into you versus brushing it off. Kaleb, we have such an age gap between us, I felt as though I didn't give you the big sister love you deserved. Kimani and Kaleb, I am so proud of the young men you both are becoming. I pray the wisdom I have shared with you, the Bible studies we have done, and the honest moments we have had will let you know how much I love you. Breona, we aren't blood sisters, but you stepped into my life as an older Sister who was willing to help me get it together. I never thanked you enough and I'm sorry. Breona, you're amazing and I am grateful that God blessed me with an older Sister who I can be honest with. I shared my broken moments with you. You were able to see the brokenness turn into beauty. Thank you for not judging me.

My dearest siblings, you have my unconditional love from this point on. We have been through these Rocky Mountains together, and I want to say thank you for loving me through my brokenness. Thank you for cheering me on to become the woman who became brave enough to write this letter.

# A LETTER TO MY MOM

*God, life for my mom wasn't easy and it's not my place to share her testimony but there was a generational curse that was creeping its way into our relationship. It wasn't your typical Mother-daughter fairytale. We struggled. I was a Daddy's girl and I didn't understand the way my mom conducted herself. God, my Mom is an amazing woman who has a BIG heart. What she lacked was self-discipline. The way she conducted herself turned her traits into family issues. She wanted us to have everything but financially my parents couldn't afford the lifestyle that she envisioned for her children.*

My Mother wanted me to be great and she pushed me hard. My Mother's determination to see the best in me was amazing, however, it never fully clicked with me. I sensed that her motive behind my greatness was to please others. She wanted me to be like other children but what she didn't understand is that I needed a relationship with her. One where she told stories of what it was like for her growing up from a young girl to a young woman. God, I wanted my Mom to be softer with me. I wanted more hugs and conversations. I wanted her to teach me the characteristics of a good wife and how to present myself like a lady. I wanted her to teach me how to cook. These were just some of the things I yearned for. I know she loves me and I never doubted that. I just wished that she would have invested in me differently. When I witnessed my

Mom enduring abusive situations, I was too wrapped up in being a Daddy's Girl that I became angry with her for being a weak woman. I was angry with her for the divorce. I was angry with her for the advice she gave me. I was angry with her for my abortion. I HATED her when my Son died.

*God, how crazy is it that I could feel a burning fire inside of my heart every time I saw her?*

This was the devil painting an image of Motherhood as purposeless. He wanted me to think less of my Mother. He wanted me to be angry and have no relationship with her.

What I should have been doing is forgiving her, embracing her knowledge, embracing her strength, encouraging her flaws, and mending our Mother/Daughter relationship. God, the devil knew that my Mother's touch was so important to me. He wanted to destroy what I needed. I became so closed off that my character and presence was aggressive and serious. Mentally I didn't want to be so hard, but I didn't know how to become soft. I believe my Mother was lost after her and my Dad's divorce. I was so angry with her that I became disrespectful towards her.

Not once did I look in her eyes and recognize the investment she made in her children by putting her dreams on hold. She wanted us to be the best by teaching us what she knew. My Mother was young when she had me. Therefore, I was considered the guinea pig baby. She was learning how to be a Mother while she was raising me. Crazy how sometimes I look back and wonder what I could have done to help make things easier for her or how I could have taken more time to understand her. People often ask me about my relationship with my Mother and I remember becoming irritated when her name would come up.

Today, I am blessed to say that the devil couldn't keep us separated. God, You convicted me in the middle of the night with a message that no matter how good my work is here on earth, if unforgiveness ruled my life, I would never step into the fullness of your heart. My tears were intense because I held on to my pain from my Mother that festered and stripped away my joy. That night, I cried to You and asked You to help me rebuild our relationship. You answered my prayer with lighting speed and told me to drive to Dallas, TX to see my Mom. When I made it there, we decided to go out for dinner. During the ride to the restaurant, I silently prayed to the Lord for strength to get through this. It had been years since my Mom and I had been on good terms and I didn't know what to expect or even what to say.

As we sat across from each other glancing at our menus, I could feel the anger stirring up in my bones. I had to quickly call out Your name in my head to change my mindset. Lord, I thank you for not allowing me to live with hatred in my heart that was merely there to stunt the growth of what you deemed as a beautiful mess.

Dear Mom, I forgive you. I am proud of you and I ask that you forgive me. I know you love poems so here is mine to you.

**Out of hatred and pain, I watched and judged you of your insecurities and closed the door on the love you had for me. I created a picture of you through your pain and considered you weak. I even changed your name from Kenya to a woman lost in the game. See, I was wrong for not seeing the true you. When I closed my eyes to block the evil spirits, I now understand how your strength was so colorful and your love so warm. I watched you**

care for four babies while you were facing crazy storms. God didn't make a mistake when He created me through you because He knew you were strong enough to take on the pain that would crush my spirit but change my name. See, Peter was Simon and Paul was Saul. They said Jesus was hypocrite, but He died for us all. God knew my life would be attacked so he birthed me through a Mother who was strong enough to have my back. You invested what you could as God knew you would.

My Dear Mother, I am sorry for not noticing the posture of you bending your back to cry was the footstool that I needed to fly. I love you.

# *A LETTER TO MY DAD*

*God, you gave me one cool Father. He's always been my best friend, but our relationship still had some trouble. My Father couldn't envision me not being great. He couldn't envision me not conquering the dream he had for me since I was a baby. I felt like I had to play sports or our relationship wouldn't hold as much value.*

My Dad worked hard for our family and failing was not an option. He was my coach and we worked out for hours and hours, practice after practice and I enjoyed it up until I entered high school. I just wanted my Father. I came from parents who put everything they had into their children because they felt like they never got an opportunity to reach their full potential. My Dad started out as a Parent who could balance the dual roles of Coach and encourager. I could talk to him about anything. That changed during my high school years.

My Dad became frustrated with his life and couldn't motivate me anymore. He couldn't show me the love he wanted to because he didn't love himself. I began to fear my Dad and didn't feel comfortable telling him things that I used to be able to tell him like, "Dad, basketball is overwhelming." My Dad handled me stopping anything I was good at as giving up, backing down, and would often enlighten me on the sacrifice that he made for us.

Pure guilt trip. I was so afraid to disappoint my Dad that I wasn't honest with my feelings.

God, my Dad had so much frustration inside that his reactions were unpredictable. I never knew what to expect. I was disappointed that his attitude was so mean, his heart had grown cold, and he stopped telling me that he was proud of me. He stopped saying that he loved me. I needed my Dad's validation, but he was in his own world. I discovered this, through a relationship I should have never been in. I told myself I would never marry anyone like my Father because I wanted true love in my marriage. I didn't witness that kind of love with my parents' marriage.

*God, when my Dad closed himself in a box he took a part of me with him.* I needed to know that my Dad wasn't going to give up on me through my storms, but he was trapped in his own. Immaturity makes you look at what you need instead of what a person is going through. My Dad is a man that has beat the odds and has created success for himself. My Father didn't grow up with the best hand dealt to him, but he has an ambitious heart that causes him to work hard. I watched joy overcome my Dad's life over the years. He traveled more, was in a new healthy marriage, built his first house, and was in a new season of excellence. I owe God and my Stepmom a thank you for that. There are days that I think about not changing my last name because I see how my

Dad turned the name Johnson from a name of pain to a new standard of joy. I want to take the Johnson legacy to a level it has never been before.

Dad: The sacrifices you made don't go unnoticed, your demanding work is appreciated, and your strength is amazing. We still disagree on my purpose sometimes, and every now and then (like every phone call) you mention some form of how I can stay connected to basketball. I love you because you are my Dad, period. The old Kyaris was immature on discerning you giving your all versus my selfish thoughts.

I am honored to say that my Dad wasn't and isn't perfect. I never realized how we get so caught up on how a person is standing that we forget to appreciate that they are just there. So, thank you for being there even when you worked forty plus hour weeks. When your back bothered you all day. Through our arguments. When it looked like my life had no chance of getting better. Thank you for showing me that life isn't easy, and that love can be perfectly imperfect. I forgive you. I am proud of you and I ask that you forgive me.

## ACTIVITY:

Remove your feelings and open your heart to being in your parent's shoes. Write down the goodness of what they did for you and hold on to the thought that they are only human. Ask them to share their upbringing with you. Ask them to open their hearts with you and listen. Pain doesn't pick and choose. We are all affected by it, but we cannot forget that taking our time to ask someone to share their story brings more clarity than assuming or saying what you would have done.

# *A LETTER TO MY STEPMOM*

Our relationship has been super confusing. I met you in between the flames of my parents' ongoing battles. I was so immature that I didn't know if I should like you, hate you, or just ignore the fact that you were even around. It was hard seeing another woman in my Dad's life. I was raised most of my life with both parents and it was difficult seeing you with my Dad. You were a woman I wanted to like for my Father and at the same time, hate you for my Mother.

I was confused as a teenager about which side I was supposed to take as I experienced the back lash, division, and broken heart of my parents' unstable situation. My parents' divorce was messy and full of hatred. There was no peace and you entering the picture only made matters worse. I felt like even with my family having ups and downs, you were a stranger. My parents weren't legally divorced, so I felt like you took the hope of my parents fixing their relationship. I also knew in my heart that chances of them fixing their relationship was slim either way. Over time and through healing, I noticed that another issue I had stemmed from jealousy. I was my Dad's little girl. Now this woman is trying to tell me she knows my Dad as well as I do, if not better than me. I loved my Dad so much I didn't really want to see anyone in the picture. When God began to heal me, I had to deal with the pain of having a Stepmom and my reservations about you. I noticed a level of immaturity on my behalf because I never really witnessed my Dad in a peaceful and joyful state. I felt like I had lost my Dad and did not want to accept that my Dad was stepping into a new side of love. A side that was way overdue.

Can I just say *"Thank You"?* I thank you for loving my Father past his flaws. Thank you for loving him into greatness and seeing me as your daughter despite our ups and downs.

## **DEAR PEOPLE WHO HAVE STEP-PARENTS:**

I get it. It isn't easy to understand, accept, or even watch your parent be with someone new. I challenge you to take some time and release the spirit of pride, anger, or the idol marriage you had for your parents and get to know the other person.

## ACTIVITY:

Take some time and really search your heart. Try to figure out what is blocking you from learning and loving the person your parent loves. As Christians, we must evaluate our heart and submit our ways to align with God's purpose for us. Once you've searched your heart and gained an understanding of why you feel the way that you do concerning your stepparent, leave it in God's hand. Now, call them, invite them out to eat and talk to them. Give them a chance to understand where your heart has been. Listen to what they have to say and allow the lines of communication for feelings to be expressed and for God to bring reconciliation.

# ATTENTION

*Dear Jesus: College was where I encountered the boiling of the brokenness and the fullness of my lost identity. Losing Ryan was my breaking point and I lost connection with the world. I went into a severe depression, spiritual death, and encountered many distractions. I tattooed my body up, got piercings in crazy places, and became a wild child. I started using men to buy my meals, pay my bills, and anything I could get out of them. I had no desire for a relationship. Deep down inside I was trapped in the hands of my ex. A relationship was the last of my worries but filling the lonely void was necessary. A warm cuddle or anything to fill the void in my life was enough for me. I remember having sex one night and crying because I knew that I lost myself, but I* wasn't sure on where I needed to start cleaning up this mess of a life I was in.

Every time I tried to come clean with myself and get back on track to loving me, it became worse and I'm not one to lie. I was a girl trapped in lust for men, liquor, weed, trap music, and clubs. I didn't want to go to class or to basketball practice. Yes, I was a college athlete who would leave the club at 3:00am to be on the court by 5:00am. Why? Because I was sneaky about my life and chaos was my new identity. Pain changed my identity and taught me how to live up to it. Pain caused a lot of damage, but secrets led my life. I perfected masking pain and my behavior to the pain. I chose to date outside of my school so that no one would know what I was doing or who I was doing it with. I had a charming demeanor to others, but I didn't have many friends. People had no clue that my insides were bleeding out joy, love, hope, identity, purpose, and forgiveness every day of my life.

With every ounce of blood slowly pouring out of your body, it's easy to welcome death. Bleeding to death is slow and all you want is to have someone notice that you're even bleeding. I had been cut to the core so many times that a bandage wasn't big enough to heal the scars of my wounds. I was judged by some, cool to others, and not seen by most. I remember being so frustrated because no one recognized my pain, not even the Mother of the church who found it amusing to judge me instead of encouraging me.

Only if someone would have taken a moment to look me in the eyes and see that my lifestyle reflected the brokenness that started at five years of age. I just wanted someone to tell me that it would all be okay. That my life had purpose, and *that I was beautiful through my pain. Instead, I imagined the whispers in church being about me not being pure, and that the people I clubbed with were dancing to the beat of their own brokenness.*

*God, I remember shaving off all my hair, dying it multiple colors, wearing clothes that didn't fit me, cursing like nobody's business, being attracted to guys who sold drugs, signing up with online dating sites, and looking for a Sugar Daddy. I can't even believe this myself but it's my truth and I will be set free. I refuse to be in bondage. I fell apart. Whenever I wanted to cry and face my reality, I realized that it was too much. There was this black cloud that had been over my life for years. I was afraid and didn't know how to begin the journey to true freedom. I wanted peace and was willing to face my truth instead of living the reality of a lie. .*

## *SAVED AND SHAPED*

*Lord, I must share this! I remember years ago I was with some of my college basketball teammates heading to the mall to find outfits for the party/club we were supposed to be attending. Who would have known that a trip to the mall would be an embarrassing and belittling moment? As we walked around the mall we head into a shoe store and I was introduced to a demonic spirit who had taken over a young man's life. He was dressed in jewelry, popularity and disgust. This man was a PIMP. A TRUE PIMP approached me and was offering me money, wanted to sleep with me and asked me to work for him! He grabs my neck in the middle of the mall and I felt so disgusted! He squeezed my neck walking me away from the group with a smile to then forcedly pushing my head to his penis. He then tells me that he was going to turn me into his prostitute. I had tears of fear falling from my face and automatically my mind thought of my years of being molested and being taken advantage of!! After this moment I knew I needed help! JESUS!! My life was so dark!*

*That night I canceled all my plans and I remember drinking and smoking myself to sleep. I sat in the bathroom and just cried in silence to keep my older sister from hearing my weakness. She thought that I was strong, and I didn't want her to know otherwise. That day I cried until I couldn't cry anymore and I just laid in my bed. I remember hearing Your voice and being so angry with You. I didn't understand why You showed up in my life after years of brokenness. I remember speaking to You with so much hatred, frustration, and anger yet You still allowed Your love and peace to flow through my heart. I called Your name for the very first time, "JESUS, can't you see that I'm broken? I really didn't trust you." To my surprise, I wasn't expecting your response.*

*My daughter, I'll walk through each trial with you and I promise to heal you. That night was the first time I felt, as I like to call it, my cuddle time with the Holy Spirit. Over the next eight months I dropped out of school, moved in with my sister, and began the sabbatical I needed. That was such a beautiful season, but it was not easy. You had me journal all the pain I could remember and every day we worked on healing. This was such a hard process for me because of the amount of time the pain had been living inside of me. The pain had taken over my bloodline and my heart. Every beat of it. I was at a place where I was only producing negative things, bad relationships, a foul tongue, and the responsibility* of it all had a negative outcome. I am so grateful, on the other hand, that You saw that my entire being was affected by the turmoil from my past. You took Your time and surgically removed and healed every piece of brokenness I carried. There's no way I could repay You for staying with me even when I didn't deserve it. I can't even explain how amazing You've been in my life. I was at a breaking point and ready to die. I lost my identity, my joy, and my purpose. I blamed myself and wanted to give up but You weren't ready for me to leave this earth. Lord, I give my heart to You and I thank You for this heart transplant. My heart was dead, and You gave me Yours. I can't thank You enough but I'm going to try.

Lord, I promise to thank You daily by seeing Your children as you created them. Not in a negative image that *keeps them in bondage to the wiles of this world. I promise to share Your name and love everywhere I go. I promise to fight for the people in bondage who can't find their strength. I promise to bring the key of Jesus to set the captives FREE!*

## TO THE PEOPLE I HAVEN'T ENCOUNTERED YET

My life had some trials that led me to rock bottom. I was at a point where I didn't think I could make it. I didn't see purpose in my life and was searching for a sign of love that would help me understand who I was. I tried everything from choosing different facets of friends, not trusting my family, hanging out at various clubs, tattooing my body, being with men, drinking alcohol and smoking weed. Nothing worked. I wanted people to understand a pain that wasn't made for them to understand. To search my soul to tell me it would be okay. To heal me with their words and actions but honestly, I had placed unrealistic expectations on people and this caused me to become more depressed. My heart needed to heal and the only person who could do that was ABBA, my Father.

Out of all the people I knew, God was the only one who understood how I felt. He could relate because He is our Father. He is so gentle and amazing. I want to prepare you for what God will do in your life when you just say yes.

**_For God so loved the world, that he gave his only Son, that whoever believes in him should not perish but have eternal life._**

## *John 3:16*

God wasn't looking for me to be cleaned up for Him. He came to me when I was under the influence and He saw me as He created me and not as the bondage I was in. I have held on to the moment when God showed Himself to me and the stage of life I was in. My story or my calling isn't for everyone. But I know I am called to place the word of God on the hearts of those that are seeking Him for a sign of love. Jesus is the best love. I don't know you but now that I've shared my story with you, I want you to know that I see you. I don't have to see your physical body to know that your heart is heavy. You may be going through some trials, struggling with pride, being overly ambitious, suffering a heartbreak, or even going through an identity crisis. I am not here to judge you. I am here to let you know that God's love can heal your soul and clean your heart. This could be the hardest yet best yes of your life. Whatever you are seeking in your life, God is right there to fill the black holes in your heart.

## *THE GIRL WHO DIDN'T KNOW - A POEM*

I know you are probably wondering, well what didn't she know?

I didn't know that my life was going to be a journey of trials.

I didn't know that these trials wanted to destroy my life.

I didn't know these trials wanted to devour my destiny and identity.

I didn't know these trials wanted me to die.

I didn't know that I would be nineteen years old crying myself to sleep because I was lost.

I didn't know that I would be in a black hole of depression.

I didn't know that my life would be broken to the point of feeling that I couldn't make it.

I didn't know God.

I didn't know how to understand others pain. I didn't know myself.

BUT GOD!

I didn't know that God would step in.

I didn't know that I would be healed.

I didn't know that God would bring me to peace.

I didn't know that God wanted to make me whole. I didn't know that God would use me.

I didn't know that I would find God and He would cleanse me.

I didn't know that God would never leave me.

I didn't know I was called for greater.

I didn't know I would graduate college. I didn't know I would have an identity. I didn't know I was strong enough.

I didn't know I would mentor men & women. I didn't know I would forgive my mom.

I didn't know I could love my Father all over again in a new way.

I didn't know I would see my stepmom as another Mother.

I didn't know I would forgive and rebuild relationships with the ones who molested me.

I didn't know I was called to preach.

I didn't know my heart could love again.

I didn't know I was assigned for the broken. I didn't know I would break family curses.

I didn't know I would be sitting here writing a book about a journey I never thought I would heal from but, yet I am writing from a place of perseverance.

**You might not know but God does. Don't stop fighting!**

## ABOUT THE AUTHOR

**Kyaris Johnson** is 24 years-old and was raised in Detroit by way of Arlington, Texas. Brought up by her parents Kimani Johnson and Kenya Watkins-Johnson, and Stepmother Paulette Johnson, she is the oldest of their four children. She holds a degree in General Studies with a focus in Psychology, and is currently pursuing a divinity degree at Houston Baptist University. Following her formal education Kyaris plans to become a Pastor, found a nonprofit for homeless children, and build a foster care center.

Her ultimate goal is to leave a footprint on the Earth by inspiring and motivating many with her natural and spiritual gifts. She seeks to do this while carrying the legacy of her Son, Ryan Allen, who passed in 2012 at just 11 months old. A highlight of her life thus far has been the moments of inspiring others with her stories of growth through Jesus Christ. Kyaris desires to not only better the people she encounters but leads them to the ultimate healer and standard of love.

Kyaris goes on record unashamedly stating that her life has been hard and a consistent battle of trials, obstacles, and heartbreak but her brokenness led her to an amazing opportunity of finding herself but most importantly Christ! ***The Girl Who Didn't Know*** is her first book.

LEARN MORE NOW AT
**PURELYPERSEVERANCE.COM**

www.ingramcontent.com/pod-product-compliance
Lightning Source LLC
Chambersburg PA
CBHW050648160426
43194CB00010B/1863